ABOUT THE AUTHOR

Kathryn O'Driscoll is a UK slam champion who represented England in the finals of the World Cup of Slam in 2021. She has performed at the Edinburgh Festival Fringe, The Royal Albert Hall, Cheltenham Literary Festival, Bath Festival, on BBC Radio Bristol, at multiple UK national competitions, and was a featured poet on the BAFTA-winning spoken word TV show Life and Rhymes. She enjoys writing, performing, teaching, curating events and facilitating community spaces for Spoken Word. She most recently became Co-Artistic Director of the PBH's Free Fringe Spoken Word Team.

www.kathrynodriscoll.com
www.linktr.ee/poetryod

Kathryn O'Driscoll
Cliff Notes

VERVE
POETRY PRESS
BIRMINGHAM

PUBLISHED BY VERVE POETRY PRESS
https://vervepoetrypress.com
mail@vervepoetrypress.com

All rights reserved
© 2022 Kathryn O'Driscoll

The right of Kathryn O'Driscoll to be identified as author of this work has been asserted in accordance with section 77 of the Copyright, Designs and Patents Act 1988.

No part of this work may be reproduced, stored or transmitted in any form or by any means, graphic, electronic, recorded or mechanical, without the prior written permission of the publisher.

FIRST PUBLISHED FEB 2022

Printed and bound in the UK
by ImprintDigital, Exeter

ISBN: 978-1-913917-02-9

Cover artwork: Kathryn O'Driscoll

For the girl who couldn't see any reason to endure another day, but did.

CONTENTS

The Theory of Relativity	14
The List	15
III	17
Lockdown, 2004 - 2012	18
Bedbound & Beyond	19
Co-Habitating	20
Roses	21
Special	22
The Little Things	24
Dorchester Hospital, 1995	25
Gangrenous	26
Toy Limbs	27
Hired Mourner	29
Anaphora	32
Laurac Le Grand, 1992	34
CPU	36
Bowl	38
Collapse	39
The Thing	40
Disorderly Conduct	42
Tracey Emin Got Nothin' On Me	44
The Recovery Position	46
Catatonia	47
The Secret of Stars	49

Before	50
Cherry Pop	51
Warm Cheddar	52
Remnants	53
The Jack-O'-Lantern	55
Clemency	56
Pomegranate	57
The Bird Bone Breaker	58
Laced	60
The Lymphatic / Emphatic System	61
Silenced	62
Consecration	64
The Pit, The Core	66
Electrical	68
Camaraderie	70
I Kiss Like Church	72
Found	73
Diminuendo	74
Nothing But	76
The Moon (Part I & II)	78
Six AM	81
The Sea	83
An Unfinished Apology	84
A Meeting	86
Nettles	88
Cemetery Flowers	90
Sunburnt	91

The Siren Song	94
A Letter to Parliament (or 'The Austere Beauty of Trying Not to Die')	96
Reassurances	98
Frenchay Hospital, 2008	99
PIP2 by the Department of Work and Pensions	100
Halo	102
The Last Light	103
Uric Acid	104
Meeting Magic	106
Growing	108
Ways of Coping With A Personality Disorder Distorting How Your Brain Processes Reality And Making You Really Fucking Miserable	109
Peony-Bruised	110

Acknowledgements

Cliff Notes

CONTENT WARNINGS

The following list is to help you navigate this collection safely. We have attempted to identify common themes, images or subjects that have the potential to cause distress so that you can choose whether or not to engage with those poems based on your own understanding of your needs. The poems that may contain these triggers are listed in the brackets, in order of their appearance within the collection.

Ableist slurs (Special).
Anti-depressants (The Siren Song).
Anxiety / disorder (Camaraderie).
Auto cannibalism (Nothing But).
Binge eating / disorder (The List, Disorderly Conduct).
Blood (Diminuendo, Nothing But).
Body Dysmorphia (The Thing).
Breathlessness (Laced, Camaraderie).
Child suffering (Dorchester Hospital, 1995, Anaphora).
Corpse (Gangrenous, Toy Limbs, Consecration, The Last Light).
Cremation (CPU, Silenced).
Death (Gangrenous, Toy Limbs, Dorchester Hospital, 1995, Hired Mourner, I Kiss Like Church, Nothing But, The Last Light).
Department of Work and Pensions (A Letter to Parliament, PIP2).
Disabled children (Special, Dorchester Hospital, 1995, Anaphora).
Dislocation (Nothing But).
Drowning (Meeting Magic).
Extreme intrusive thoughts (Consecration).
Eye damage (Nothing But).
Falling from a height (Catatonia).
Funeral imagery (Gangrenous, Toy Limbs, Hired Mourner, CPU, Consecration, I Kiss Like Church).
Governmental abuse (A Letter to Parliament, PIP2).
Insects (The List, Co-Habitating, Consecration, I Kiss Like Church).
Loss (Special, Gangrenous, Toy Limbs, Hired Mourner, Anaphora, CPU, The Last Light).

Medical abuse (Special, A Letter to Parliament, Frenchay Hospital, 2008, PIP2, Reassurances).
Minor injury (Before).
Medical imagery / language (The Lymphatic / Emphatic System, The Last Light, Uric Acid).
Oppression of disabled people (A Letter to Parliament, PIP2).
Panic attacks (Camaraderie).
Physical harm (Nothing But).
PTSD (Remnants, The Jack-O'-Lantern, Clemency, Pomegranate, The Bird Bone Breaker, Electrical, I Kiss Like Church).
Rape – description or metaphor of act (Warm Cheddar, Consecration).
Rape – discussion (Before, Cherry Pop, Remnants, The Bird Bone Breaker, Consecration).
Rape – implication (The Jack-O'-Lantern, Clemency, Pomegranate, Laced, Electrical, I Kiss Like Church).
Rivers (An Unfinished Apology, A Meeting, Nettles, The Siren Song, A Letter to Parliament).
Political abuse (A Letter to Parliament, PIP2).
Self-destructive behaviours (The List, Camaraderie, Nothing But, Nettles).
Self-harm (Co-Habitating, The Thing, Nothing But, Nettles).
Self-loathing (The Thing, The Pit, The Core).
Sexual assault – description or metaphor of act (Warm Cheddar, Consecration).
Sexual assault – discussion (The Bird Bone Breaker, Consecration).
Sexual assault – implication (Before, Cherry Pop, Remnants, The Jack-O'-Lantern, Clemency, Pomegranate, Silenced, Laced, Electrical, I Kiss Like Church, Meeting Magic).
Shame (I Kiss Like Church).
Slugs (Remnants).
Snake (Hired Mourner).
Spiders (Six AM).
Suicidal ideation (The List, Bedbound & Beyond, Co-Habitating, An Unfinished Apology, A Meeting, Nettles, Sunburnt, The Siren Song, A Letter to Parliament, Halo, Frenchay Hospital, 2008).
Suicide attempt/s description (An Unfinished Apology, A Meeting, Nettles, The Siren Song, A Letter to Parliament, Halo, Frenchay Hospital, 2008).

Suicide attempt/s discussion (An Unfinished Apology, A Meeting, Nettles, Sunburnt, The Siren Song, A Letter to Parliament, Halo, Frenchay Hospital, 2008, Meeting Magic).
Systematic oppression (A Letter to Parliament, PIP2).
Traffic collisions (Clemency).
Victim blaming (I Kiss Like Church, Sunburnt).
Vomit (Tracey Emin Got Nothin' On Me).
Wounds (Cherry Pop, Silenced, Frenchay Hospital, 2008).

Cliff Notes

The Theory of Relativity

Trudging through suction-mud fields,
a thousand cheese wire strings
wrapped around every limb,
I pull a cloud
in caravan behind me,
it tugs - an abrupt parachute drag,
caught on a storm, then sinks,
sullen, into the ground
and I can't move forward.

A whisper whips across my face
      'how heavy could the sky *be?*'

The List

After Caroline Bird

My diagnosis is a flight of birds for a heart.

My diagnosis is one ear underwater.

They caught me licking the different metals of pylons,
trying to shock my system back to stupor.

My diagnosis is an exaggeration of everything.
Phone pings are confetti canons in library-quiet graveyards.

They caught me leaning over the edge.

My diagnosis is the crawling of insects
that sneak into orifices when I sleep,
relax, kiss, forget about *him*.

They caught me filling holes with food
to make myself a fortress,
oversized, brickwork groaning.

My diagnosis is deadly company.
They took that half of me away, cremated it,
I keep expecting my right arm to comfort me.

My diagnosis is silt in the blood, pooling in joints.

My diagnosis is hyper-attentiveness
to the whereabouts of the teeth of smiling omnivores.
They insist they do not intend on eating me.

My diagnosis is an overdose
of reality
and a tenderness towards sharp objects that appear
closer in the mirror.

My diagnosis is I deserve this.

III

It's the third day in a row that the world has ended.
The smog's so thick we can't see mushroom clouds anymore,
but we feel them.
Shaken to our bunker cores
our hearts palpitate a funeral march.
We hack up smoke particles, each cough a sonic boom,
we cry sand.

There's nothing but rib racks shaking,
and eyes, bleached by the sun's explosion,
still staring out into the noise for hope.
There's nothing but the concrete
trapping us in stasis.
Barely breathing,
dying,
already dead.

Lockdown, 2004 – 2012

You will relocate your jaw bones and call me
in a month when your world rightens again.
I will be hung upside down, planted on the ceiling,
socially distanced from anything grounding.
I can't reach the phone right now, please call back later.
Prayers circulate my personal chapel of lonely:
please, call back, the walls echo. I won't want to speak
when you're back in your great wide everywhere else
and I'm still stuck here. But call me back. You know
where to find me. Lying foetal around the lightbulb
swinging shadows around the room as if I'm spinning
at the centre of a beautiful party.

Bedbound & Beyond

Daylight's breadth plugged with plastic
sheets and sticky tape.
Windows brim full of invasion,
I try to hold it back.
The light gets through anyway,
disturbing my brief relief.

I stare at the wall waiting for the dark
in me to eat the sun again.

I imagine the mould as branch-like fingers.
Damp as new life
seeping through the walls to try and embrace me.
Rather than just my own condensation trying, as I am,
to escape by the means of little rivers
and rot.

Co-Habitating

Flies splay a constellation in reverse
across the wardrobe door sky.
They thrum and gossip at the smell of blood.
Their wet little feet patter every surface.
Tiny black hearts ache to take my kingdom
if only the knife would slip -
they buzz excitedly as I wretch into their airspace.
They don't want to share this room with a human anymore.
I grasp for the precious edge of sanity
or the very corner of a steady breath
                             - someone knocks
What am I doing? Thinking about feeding the flies.

Roses

I brought you roses

and came back each day,
to watch them decaying

and tried not to liken them
to your body beneath the earth.

Special

My sister
came with a free soundtrack.
Mottled purple but still beautiful,
she cried for seven hundred and thirty-six days straight.

The doctors told my parents she wouldn't live
past two.

My sister
clung to me with clammy, happy hands,
threw crayons and books in my direction,
signed to me: *food*,
and when the crying drowned down
to a drizzle at the back of her throat,
sometimes she laughed.

The doctors told my parents she would suffer.
That she'd be chair bound with nerve endings on fire until
someone snuffed her out.

My sister
liked kisses and Weetabix made soggy
from the milk. She liked to play with hand bells
and always spilled her drinks. She liked to race
her electric wheelchair past the kitchen table
and steal my Daddy's wine.
(Sometimes he laughed).

My sister
did walk – with help.
She blew the impact of her life into shrapnel stars

so I always have guidance home. She became the sky for me.

My sister
    the *fucking*
    spastic
    retard.

    Spastic.
Yeah. Spastic.
Skeletal muscles contracting without control. Yeah.

    Retard.
Yeah. Retarded.
Someone who's brain development occurred slower than average.
Maybe even limited.
That's what it means. That's all that it means.
It means when your baby sister is squirming
in pain as her organs turn cartwheels you can't explain
to her why it hurts so much.
It means crying – she's crying, I'm crying –
it means agony.

    Fucking.
Yeah, fucking - that's my fucking sister.
And I've heard people call her,
or friends,
or enemies by names they synonymise with offense
and sometimes I laughed.
Trying not to be unreasonable about language.
Cos if you don't know what it's like to hold your sibling in your arms as they writhe, wriggling closer to death because
they don't understand why you don't love them enough to make the pain stop –
good for you.

23

The Little Things

When I was a child the term 'rose gold'
didn't exist. But when I try to remember you,
I only see the side of your cheek,
the plump curve of a hill in a plain of peach
mixed with milk, and your hair,
lit like seraphim strands by the sun.
Every memory of you is tinged with it,
the honeyed glaze of a carnation budding
just before it is cut
and pressed between the pages of a book
to turn brown.

Dorchester Hospital, 1995

I can't forget the yellow handrails in Dorchester Hospital. Spread out like wings as you walk to the paediatric unit. I can't forget the rust bricks, I did not know the colour of blood then. I can't forget the grass, perched timidly at the foot of the building. The desire to crush it with my feet.

The curtains flushed blue; how our whole street lit up. I can't forget soft pink pillowcases that smelled like grandparents, like safety. Her hair tickling my cheek, feather-light and gossamer. I can't forget her cheek, my small damp hands struggling to hold her body as she screamed.

Gangrenous

The bloated tongue escapes the ephemeral and lifts
skyward – stuck in a congealed throat,
draped with the closed curtains of bile and blood
souping a dam across her vocal chords. No words.

The hair is brushed, later, out of its nooseloops
until it is straight and lies flush with the velvet
in a box, just big enough to bury the dreams
of a life lived without pain.

The chemicals of her unusually sewn body,
combine in a way geneticists cannot explain
to exude the only smell it can. Of her. But
it is no longer the familiar, the warmth of milk dust.
Now acids boil together to purge.

The familiarity of her fades funereal
and only the rotting of her organs,
which had laid undetected in her gut for months
reminds us she is one and the same;
the clay lump that was once a sister.

Toy Limbs

The white plastic body
of a My Little Pony
impervious to organ failure
has her toy limbs bent
in aesthetically pleasing
and anatomically correct poses
that do not require splints
or physiotherapy.
Frazzled plastic hair
with I.V. injected colour
that shouts!
against silenced skin
as she is pressed into the box,
snug with the silkworms
and the soiled velvet.
Another bleached-white body,
also now impervious to organ failure,
with its own toy limbs bent
into the illusion
of an aesthetically pleasing
and anatomically
correct peace.

ALL I AM
ALL I AM
GOOD FOR
HERE FOR
ALL I AM FOR
IS
REMEMBERING
YOU

Hired Mourner

I.

I cry when the box is buried,
when the flowers are burnt away,
when the others cry.

I cry for so long that a thick Uncle's chins wobble
with the concern of having to pay me overtime.

Only when I have cried so hard
that even those who paid me have become alarmed
at my grief,
only when I hear *How sad, it must be. To feel
loss so deeply.*
How beloved, the dead! whispered behind gloved hands,
only then, when even the leaseholders of my
lamentations are fooled,
do I stand.
Slowly fold up my chair, return it to the gravedigger,
get back in my car and go home.

I feed the cash to my snake,
drop coins into its terrarium so it clinks when it tries
to go to bed,
and then I cry some more.

II.

I show up promptly on time, step into the cemetery,
let the creaking arms of this holy place hold me.
I cry on cue.

I cry when they ask me to.
I tuck lilies into all of my pockets and as the ceremony
fades into the wake,
I smell like the crush of them in all the seams of me.

I've been to so many funerals for this family now
that some of the cousins are beginning to recognise me.
One tried to pass me a curling cucumber sandwich
and tells me it's a terrible shame.

A confused friend of the deceased's girlfriend pays me.
He isn't sure they hired me for this one, but is too
awkward to ask.

In the car I chew on the bank notes,
it muffles the sound of me still crying as the car park
empties.

III.

They have stopped paying me for my services.

IV.

They ask the priest to make me leave,
but I know this family now
as well as they know the sound of my long slick hearse
arriving.
You trusted me to remember the dead on your behalf
and now you expect me to just let go?
This is what you wanted, wasn't it?
The violence of a woman ripped open?
You wanted someone to paint the portrait of loss
so that you didn't have to look at it for too long yourselves?

I get into the coffin with Great-Aunt Esme and hold her,
tell her stories of how loved her family were,
how much I wept when they were lost.
Her son Steve shouts something like, *this is a disaster!*

Yes, I think. You're right.
That's what grief should feel like. A disaster.
Finally.

I am thrown from the church by a friend
of Steve's who works in security.

I don't know how they will live
without me.

Anaphora

Will this poem be how you meet her?

Origami of a girl folded into a faded red leather wheelchair frame.

Cackling in sunlight, throwing back her head, the movement of goldslips of hair curled like the honeyed drawl in the word 'Louisiana'.

Open the door of Number One, Four Acre Close and see her splayed out in the hallway surrounded by plasticine and a sippy cup. I dare you not to smile.

Rolling like a country song beat across the living room carpet to reach a favoured toy / a glass of wine / car keys that make the good noise when they jingle together.

In the back of the Rover in Carcassone, pulling the soft white out of the centre of a baguette. See how the crust turns into a long bracelet her arm has become trapped in. Hear how sisters shriek together when they laugh.

Will you hold her upright, her back against your chest, her heartbeat knocking. Will you answer?

Face and hands sticky, wriggling, yoghurt-covered sibling. The trails of dribble out of a gummy mouth, hung open, happy to see you.

Clapping, ringing handbells, throwing soft-cover children's books, listening to the tenth round of 'four little monkeys, jumping on the bed', eye-rolling, more laughing, playdoh, Weetabix and turning to gangrene inside.

Will this be what keeps her alive?
Brown eyes warm as childhood memory.

Did I get it right this time? Did you see her?

Laurac Le Grand, 1992

Euphoric daughter
on a balcony that teeters at a 20-degree angle
tipped towards crash
through too-thin railings.
Beside my sister whose wheelchair has to be
parked at a right angle to the drop.
Clambered into my father's lap
demanding his full attention,
I show him my painting
of the Southern Pyrenees baked terracotta.
He tells me all about perspective.

Well, the truth is,

I rely on this precious fragment
of my past to stay untouched.

A doting sister.
Fetching beakers full of squash, bibs, plasticine,
depositing them on the clip-on plastic tabletop
that attached to Laura's wheelchair.
The day spills sticky over all other memories.
Amberglass and honey slow, this day
remains like drinking syrup.
My Dad taught me how to paint
the view spread lazily below the railings

and this is a happy memory.
But,

on the pitch of disaster,
more than once
the wheels slowly rolled towards those railings.
And now I have to force myself to remember
all the times we did
manage to catch her.

CPU

I've left too many tabs open for grief
I can hear music playing quietly in my
subconscious
and you're going 'yeah yeah yeah',
and there's pictures of you smiling,
and a picture of us hugging, 30 years ago,
and there's your obituary,
and the florist,
and google maps,
and the menu for the crematorium restaurant,
and I don't want anything out of an oven
and I feel sick.

And I am slow, and full, and I crash easily;
because you left so suddenly;
mid way through using my CPU -
my thoughts full of you and that hospital
room.

And all the tabs are left Unclosed.
And all the static keeps interrupting,
and the music is either a complex instrumental
too inventive
for me to understand
or the same truth playing over and over,
and I don't want it to be a dirge.
I don't want to write a eulogy.
I will leave that tab blank and at the back.
I will close and reopen it.
I will pretend.

I will get overwhelmed and the world will crash abruptly into
slow motion
again
because my brain is overloaded.
And yes it's just 'one thing'.
Just one more box to buy,
one more body to burn,
one more goodbye to memorise.
But it's not just one thing.

It's a person.

And my mind cannot filter, or organise
or close down the truths about you that I am not ready to let go
of yet.

So I burn out.
And I cry when I see coffee cake.
And I open a new tab and write a note
'Reminder. Learn how to Forget how to make coffee cake'.

Bowl

Coolness sifts through my gills,
slipping through my scales, pushing
against my fins. No matter which way
I turn there is always more water.
'I've never been in this part of the bowl
before,' I think, 'at 4.34 on a Tuesday.'
The light hits differently each time.
Sometimes the water is barely there,
a thin cornea between me and the world,
sometimes it holds me, constricts,
murky and bleak. This too is new.
As a goldfish, my sole job is to observe.
I even admire the stream of bubbles
that run upward, away, as I die. Huh,
I don't remember seeing that before -
that explosion of air.

Collapse

All cracked foundations, subsidence,
sagging plasterboard swollen with bath water,
the ceiling coming down,
caving in.

All wet window-ledges, rot in the frames,
wood warping from weeping.
All sewage pipes backing up.

More hovel than home,
more termite teeth than fortress wall.

I am not a safe place.

The Thing

Downstairs,
in the wardrobe partially blocked
by the wide hips of a rocking chair,
I keep my body.

Occasionally,
when the dust motes dance
in great golden slashes through my living room,
I visit it.

Wrangle it out.
The house holds its breath.
A sheaf of flesh bent double over a coat hanger,
I brace myself.

Hold it
between me and mirror. Flatten with hands.
Don't think about Louisiana swamplands expanding.
I double in size.

I try
to think of curves as catching points for embraces,
this arm crook is where my fiancé's crown falls,
I am a landscape of possibility,

Jabba the Hutt,
slugs' skin dried and stretched,
a yard of peach latex, wibbling as it's cut.
I pierce it.

Another hole,
needle sized, beneath the fingernails,
behind the ears, under the droopy eyelids,
I pierce it.

Here, here and here
and this is the same as losing weight, right?
Holding myself like an evidence bag,
I pierce it.

Shove back to darkness
refuse to look at it again all winter.
My mirror is all metaphor,
I cover it with silk.

Disorderly Conduct

The moon is molten
with a sunray-thin custard skin
confining it globular as it hangs, ripe.
I'm going to pluck the moon.

Squeezing satellites until they burst,
running laviacle vein-routes down my palms
and creating forest fires in my elbow pits;
I won't care. I'm going to crush the moon.

Plush inside,
rich and overly vanilla
compared to the searing cinnamon of the Sun.
I am going to eat the moon.

With teeth sunk through cellular veils,
with Saturn's rings dug into bloodied gums
and Plutonian cavities,
I will destroy the moon.

If I digest a planetary system,
intestinalise stardust,
and choke on the pulsation of a supernova,
if I eat the universe, the world, the moon -

maybe then
I'll be full.

STOP
EATING
& STOP
EATING
& STOP
EATING
& STOP
EATING
& STOP
EATING

YOU ARE SO DISGUSTING

YOU CAN BE FULL BUT YOU'LL NEVER BE WHOLE

Tracey Emin Got Nothin' On Me

and then
I cut my toenails,
blinked twice for no,
lay on the floor
and made a snow angel
out of soggy tissues
and cutlery
and burst acrylic paints
oil slicking the floorboards blue.
and then I exhaled for five,
pressed my palm against wallpaper
cut my palm on its peeling,
took off my clothes
for the first time all week
and laid them out neatly
on top of the half-filled coke cans
that spewed mould spores when moved.
and then I sneezed into a towel,
scratched my calf until it bled
and let my sheets turn copper.
I sat cross legged on the mattress
and thought about broken springs
and bit the inside of my cheek
and my fingernails
and my fingers
and the cut on my hand.
and then I vomited into my bed
curled up in it,
pretended warmth and comfort
were the same thing,

and then I died
and then I painted the room black,
and then
I cut my toenails.

The Recovery Position

How wonderful it is to go backwards!

To reverse smoothly into a parking bay
so that when you return you can drive forward
and away.

Or to fly backwards, a hummingbird to what is coming,
rejoicing.
How people smile at one walking backwards!

The art of coming home and finding the lights
still on.
Slotting back into your life where you left it.

and
oh, what poems the past could be,
if I could live through it again.

Catatonia

I slip through a quarantined city,
slow as a lidocained tongue into the hole of a pulled tooth.
A seagull squawks its warning
into the echo of deserted streets,
blusters up into the cloud cover, frightened of its own noises.
The aimless drift of kebab wrappers across cobblestones
makes the sound of a dry brush on canvas.

I cough outside a boutique.
Slack-jawed, I stare into my eyes reflected in my eyes
reflected in my eyes,
I blink and it's tomorrow again.
A tree has dropped its skirt of scentless flowers to the floor.
Brazen nudity.

I find enough stumble in my feet to keep moving
but all the shop names are blurry,
vague estimations of shape
except the glass door of a quaint café
that I try to read the menu through.
Longing. Longing. Longing. In every size.
I am already full of that.

Spinning slow in the noose-slip silence,
arms wide enough to hold a city in a loving chokehold.
Inhale an empty city's crisp air.
Eyes shut, imagine falling
towards the punch into the pavement.
Is this something I should mention to my doctors?

I reopen my eyes and I am back
at the bottom of the silent market street
The seagull pitches into the sky with a shared scream.
I bite my tongue so hard,
my mouth fills with freshly minted pennies

and I lie amid the parking tickets and mulch.
Watch the seasons drip off the façade of the Hippodrome.

The Secret of Stars

Suspended
billions of lightyears
from each other.

Hanging orbital,
silent
around skeletal
frameworks of aching.

Light fingers
desperately stretching
to try and reach
each other.

Failing.

This is why some stars fall;
the weight.

Before

Before the Macarena
Before MTV sexualised eating lollipops
Before I bought my first pair of jeans
Before dial up and downloadable ring tones
Before calling 0800 numbers from payphones
Before hanging up and running and running
Before we spilled blue raspberry Panda Pops everywhere
Before we crashed from the sugar high
Before I fed your Tamagotchi for you because you forgot
Before I told myself I would forgive you for that
Before Impulse body spray and roll on lipgloss
Before you stopped being gloriously fourteen forever
Before I borrowed your brand new rollerskates
Before flying too fast downhill
Before I fell and some part of me just kept going
Before you never said sorry
Before the streetlights came on
Before the school counsellor asked what happened
Before we made memories that are now painful by association
Before I met him
Before I taught myself CPR and resuscitated my body
Before the scar tissue and the bloodstains
Before your Tamagotchi died
Before you didn't even notice
Before you married him anyway
Before we called it rape

Cherry Pop

I fold it down small and slip it into the wedding favour;
a gauzy organza bag full of sugared almonds.
Halfway through the night I've lost track of it.
Swapped for a half-finished glass of champagne.
Hands in my hair and closed eyes to dance,
I don't even want to *think* about my body.

Outside, chugging a soft drink,
a homebound kid drops it back into my lap.
Wrapped in a napkin to stop blood soaking the bag.
There it is.
I tip the mangled circle of my flesh into my palm,
it catches the moonlight in a jagged red smile.
I stub a cigarette out on it, call a taxi.

Blood and marriage, both require sacrifice...
I tell my new fiancée later.
    Not like that, she says,
rinsing the wound in antiseptic years too late.
I curl up to sleep on the rug
ignoring the bed with its cradle cushions,
its nightstand with a glass of water, some loose paracetamol
and my own self, in a trinket dish,
turning the colour of something borrowed.

Warm Cheddar

He is a fat, oily man
with sodden palms and upper lip
who sweats profusely
onto the furnishings,
leaving his sock-stench to bloom there
before sluggishly pressing his bulbous body down,
oozing over your flesh,
grasping for a quick, cheap thrill
and falling asleep wetly beside you.

Remnants

The slug trails glug down the tripfalls of my sheets,
a silver lining.

Tiny broken sparrow bones, blood clots and lost hair
matted down into a nest
but your stench rolls fog over every fold and fibre,
and for years after, other birds refuse to come home.

I live without singing.
Without feather-touch or wing-beat light.
I live without flight.

I am starving to death.

Each time a part of me dies I make bedding from it,
I make a resting place amongst the eggshell fragments
of everything you left behind broken.

I pluck slugs off the cotton, bury down
amid their wet mouths,
make peace with yet another predator
and decay.

SHOULD HAVE LIKED IT

FOUGHT BACK HARDER
SAID IT LOUDER
EVERYONE LOVES SEX
WHAT'S WRONG WITH
HOW MANY OTHERS WERE THERE?
YOU SHOULD HAVE TOLD
HE DIDN'T MEAN TO
HE SAID HE WAS SORRY
FILTHY

The Jack-O'-Lantern

I miss my innards.
Since he took them I'm always guts trailing in crowds,
the gunshot afterthought speech breaking
hard against the soundscape:
me too, me too, me too.

If he hears, will I become his night horrors in return?
Is that what I want? For whole cities to burn
or just to be able to exhale without the fear
of snuffing myself out?

The light in my eyes is not natural.
I'm only setting fires in the chasms
he carved out of me.

I am dying
to be more than just a cautionary tale

glowing in the dark: *Beware.*

Clemency

Thumb nail stabbed into goose-bumped rind,
pried back. Exposure,
skin torn from membrane
that shivers as it snaps.

Segment wrenched,
pulled from its socket,
a missing tooth,
the orange dribbles.

Juice tries to cling on,
like tenuous synapses still firing
when neurons lie shredded
on concrete after traffic collisions.

Years later, starving, we press our faces to glass
as oranges glow in the supermarket light
as if rot is impossible.

Pomegranate

My silence is an overripe fruit,
seeping through my fingers.

I put wet fingers between my teeth,
the juice tastes the same
even from someone else's sorrow.

How many times have I bit my tongue
and been flushed sour?
Spat seeds where I hope they won't grow.

There is too much to talk about,
and not enough of me left to say it.
Nothing but lies turned liquid.

I try not to notice people
with net bags of orange and lime
tied around their necks, hung in front,
entering every room before them

averting their eyes from greengrocers,
the burn of citric acid in their throat.
The burst and bloom of shame.

The Bird Bone Breaker

My mother taught me not to take distressed birds home.
No matter how well-meaning I thought my touches to be, to
another animal, I was a giant
painting victimhood onto its back.
Tarring feathers with the unfamiliar,
baptising it into Otherness.

Don't touch the nests. Eggs. Babies.

Do not leave them with a saucer of milk and the stench of
sweat all over them
that felt like kindness but lingers like shame.
We are not saviours in every story in which we save someone.

Spurned a wingspan away from love, birds die,
asphyxiated on rejection.
Small mouths overfull of words too big for them to explain
what happened to them.

They're marked now.
Odd-smelling bird.
Cursed bird.
Make a nest of not-belongings, bird.

You
taught me not to take destructive boys home.
No matter how sweet seeming I think their touches to be.

You taught me to pay attention to the impact of hands,
wonder why caresses can curse,
well-intentioned fingerprints end up on crime scenes -
but no one ever taught you not to touch what isn't yours
without permission, did they?

You snapped my sparrow bones with too-big fingers
and I had to make myself a sleeping place
from the shards of my cartilage-cage insides
that still smell
like unwashed hands gone wandering,
long after
I chewed out the marrow and licked the bones
stained with the palest reminders of you,

raping me
so
thoughtfully,
and with all the love you could hold in your careful,
revolting hands.

Some people never learn.

I bet you think you saved the birds.

Laced

The word victim
is corset laced around me.
I feel the boning, long, slick
like men's fingers pressed into me.
I become pinched. Breaths stilted.

I would blame myself
for being on the street after dark,
but I was at home once the streetlights came on.
I was at home.
In bed. In love.
In time I will cut myself free of clothes
the weight and size of fifteen-year-old me.

I will fill my lungs with air until I am fat with it.
Until my torso shivers like the moment before bursting.

I will take the deepest breath in, keep expanding with oxygen
instead of self-loathing, until the clothing rips apart on my cue

and I will reclaim the space that I live in and oh
              – the *noise* that you will hear from me then.

The Lymphatic / Emphatic System

Everything is working correctly.
My brain is draining excess protein build-ups out,
cerebrospinal fluids through the base of the skull
and into the meningeal lymphatic vessels.

It's absorbed into my blood,
but that just means everything is working correctly.

The liver organises platelets from platitudes
and strips blood clean into two groups: spoiled and not.
It sends reassurance to my heart that we are still healthy
and that everything left is working correctly.

This is a filtration system designed to withstand.
Every organ designed to displace, to survive.

The kidneys are hardiest. They've seen the worst of me.
Skin infections from self-inflictions
but they too are working correctly.
Flushing away glucoses, salts, acids.

But despite these interwoven drainage networks,
all working as they should be,
siphoning toxins out of my bloodstream,
somehow, I'm still left with
you.

Silenced

He ripped [   ] voice right out.

Dug behind my [   ] cords, prized [   ] the ligaments
until they threatened [   ] collapse
like a fifteen-[   ]-old girl
who [   ] to call anything 'love'.

It was [   ] years until the swelling went [   ] enough
to start to swallow the [   ] of shame.

It would have been [   ], perhaps,
if I had kept the wound [   ] .
Instead, the antithesis of healing, another [   ] put his
sticky fingers down my [   ] trying to pull the music out
or [   ] least see if he could [   ] me to gag [   ] technicolour.

I have their claw marks pinstriping my [   ].
I am still swallowing my own blood,
I don't think I can [   ] it.
I can't stop my body digesting the [   ]slide of revulsion
[   ] from the site of infection.
Its spread has started to [   ] with my spinal cord:
Me and P[   ]SD.
I am wrapped up in it
and say things like: '[   ] could have been [   ]'.

I would love to see these [   ] turn to a smoke pillar
rising to meet him like a threat.
Make me a bonfire that spits at God,
with the quiet fitz fitz;
he will know it means [   ] *you*.

I wish I could tell you that lately I've been taking long walks by the beach and screaming.
I haven't been

but I am learning.

Consecration

You still lick your lips when you think of me.
Cheap Saturday strawberry gum, sunshine
on your tongue, the aftertaste of something
curdling. Waking to the midnight scene: you
at the funeral, smirking through the eulogy.
Candles drop ash and salt, purging the pews.
The choke of incense reminding – how you
held my No under holy water. Told me love
meant sacrifice. I prayed to be worth sacrifice.
May your home always smell like my body
is still there, rotting. This body you wanted
bad enough to take from me. You didn't need
consent to fill this corpse with maggots;
I don't need your blessing to haunt you with it.

YOU FEIGN PRAYER

THANKING GOD YOU RAPED ME WHEN I WAS STILL TOLERABLE LOOKING

The Pit, The Core

Cutting cherries open with a hunting knife,
peeling back the skin, exposing the tooth inside,
slicing a canal to the core, spiking the pit
and pulling it through the splayed flesh
and putting that tiny stone into a hot mouth -
doesn't despair taste like kidney stones?

Doesn't depression crunch like bruised fruit?
Doesn't blood well in the mouth like an apology
but you spit the stone into the wilderness
and it is not a pearl, is it?
It is not beauty coagulating around grit,
It is not trauma becoming a masterpiece
becoming a palatable coffee table art book
becoming a housewarming gift.
The stone is a promise.

You think this is bad?
So much more is to come.

And you spit and you spit and you spit
and you wake up in the night with the juice
slipping down from lip to ear, sticky as regret,
slinking like the truth from the shadows.
and your mattress is studded with necrotic stars
contracting after light
back to dark pits you keep finding everywhere you try to walk.

You know the truth.
You throw the cherries away,

burn them to cinder,
swear off fruit forever,
But one day you wake suddenly
and find yourself a forest of rotting food
and of course you try to throw yourself away.

Of course you do.

Electrical

Sometimes I think the sky must be an ex of mine
because of the way it presses down on me
until I cannot *breathe*
and sometimes I cry when She touches me.

Misfiring neurons like an electrical glitch.

Sometimes Her lips taste like he's haunting me.

Her kisses like an ink stamp of the reverse
of the words, 'I love you', and I have to remind Her
I didn't learn to read that way.

So quickly the intentions of the alphabet unravel
between Her tongue and my skin, [glitch]
becoming ink-smudged beyond recognition.

The same letters
can be used for lying, hurting, loving, raping, for begging–
What is wrong with me?

She tells me she loves me, and I cry
at my inability to comprehend two different [glitch] languages
of intent. It all sounds the same to me.
Sometimes I think 'I love you' sounds so much like 'please don't
hurt me'.

She says, 'you can talk to me'.

I find myself shaking. [I cannot *breathe*] [I glitch]
Don't let him touch me. Don't let him [glitch] me. [an elec].
Don't [presses down] [skin] [*please*] [sorry] [sorry] –

                                                             Sorry.

Camaraderie

cu rves and tren ches   unspooli ng   un rave lling   br eath
spiked   the shar pness of fr ost bite   numb and ne ttling   *are*
you ?   d on't touch!   skin alarm   nails exc avating half-m oons
cortisol   goosefe athers thrown   glass candlestick cracks   I
am an impact   siren   blue lig hts thwacking against
windowpanes   are you awake yet   are you alert yet   *yet?*
form ula 1 car   collapses   into confetti against the barricade
ribs   this is how an explosion lasts forever   eyes tight as jam
jar   virgin supernova   *shut it out   focus on your breath*   in case
of emergency   break   glass is not fri end   do not hold it so
close   adrenalin   anaphylaxis   throat is your secret   hold on
tight   Burden   fists slammed   filthy whore *hold on*   smashing
my head against wrought iron   metal to skull   heart spasmodic
ready for arrowhead   the violence of the thought   ready   ready
a dog's ear, a folded triangle.   soft   smooth with grain   soft   a
piercing through the back of lung   *glass of water?*   only half   no
spill   a sip   cool the vagus nerve   cool down   calm. Pillows
arranged around the shape of a fluctuating panic.   stupid organs
continuing   should cease   should fail under immense
pressure   tissue grenade everywhere   face leaking   gagging
at the texture   wet on my lip   can't cope   too gross   can't
breathe   can't   can't
                     Do you want to talk about it?   Cannot talk
words turn tongue to haybale   choking thick
disorderly letters - a whimper.   *Look at me.*   Cannot look.
Can't you tell I'm braced against the air?
I look   She signs to me.   British Sign Language.   *W. A. T. E. R?*
tilts head.   Another sip.

I allow myself to sag   to become only a hand petting a dog's head. *Just breathe, we can talk it all out later.*
My fist circles over my heart; sorry.   Sorry.   I'm sorry.

She lies down beside me, takes my sorry hand, holds on.
She pulls the blanket up. Keeps the battlefield warm.
Exhaustion.   Surrender.   Sleep.

Surrend|

I Kiss Like Church

By that I mean, with all the solemnity of a funeral incoming.
All the tension hanging from the vaulted ceiling
of a body, dangling between us. It is my body
dripping Catholic sin onto the polished stone
it is pooling in the grout lines, it is spreading.
I'm struggling to breathe amid all the incensed fury;
    I can't believe you ruined God's work,
        look at you, Body-between-us, all sticky and stinking of him.
The Bible might call me a sinner
but it doesn't really matter.
Flickering between bread and flesh
either way I am to be eaten;
I have stopped hoping to be forgiven
for his gluttony.

I dream of being a burst of flora on the altar
but when I close my eyes I see death
hiding behind met mouths.
To kiss and not think about maggots pouring. That's the dream.
But there is no daydreaming in church.
Only confession and the realisation that nothing
is resolved just because you told the air your secret.
I am humming our song, the only hymn I trust,
and you hold me like faith.
But even sacred things can become weapons
whether you believe in them or not.
Wherever we kiss, the floor is always wet like this.
I hold on too tight. I almost fall again.

Found

Hunter green bleeding over night-owl noir.
A mildewed woodland marsh with soggy bark and shuddering voices.

Here, limbs dip low with the drapery of weeds
and unwanted violence blooms a red splash on the floor,
a whimper, a goodnight.

Fog rolls heavy off my tongue, each breath a burden.
I am a wallowing, heaving place.
The moon doesn't remember my name.

I clog throats and tempers with the stench of a century caught
still; like a boy with two hands cupped over a glassed moth.
Kill all that is left fluttering with the dark.

>   She,
>   a ghost as clean as bone,
>   is lighting pin-prick candles in
>   wind-safe jars
>   along a pathway from the marshland of me
>   all   the   way
>   back
>   home.

Diminuendo

After Sean Bonney

You do not notice the great city of your mind slowing gradually.

I look out of the window in a high rise, through the Perspex sheeting, at this city stiffened up and remember the first oddities. The day all the phone towers turned into Christmas trees, but we couldn't call our Mums and tell them how wonderful it was because there wasn't any signal so we sang karaoke on the balconies. Jagged Little Pill feels just like a mother's righteousness anyway.

When all the public fountains turned off it didn't matter too much. When they replaced them all with statues of famous men sleeping, I missed the gossip of water as I made my way to work but just changed my route. Avoiding Jeff Goldblum In Linen in exchange for more trees and enough time to listen to Billie Eilish's Happier Than Ever.

I didn't mind the factories closing. Over there, in the West. From here I can see the hills behind, that used to be a glaze of smoke. Conjunctivitis of the view. I was pleased. I thought: how good. Now I'll be able to see the stars. And then I never looked.

Losing the radio disorientated me more than anything else. I'd gotten used to imagining newsreaders faces. I'd grown so fond of their smiles, or my imaginings their smiles, or the way that my imaginings of their smiles made me feel. Without that I was spaceman, walking out into the nothing. The night that Taylor Swift was dismantled and shipped somewhere safer, I cried for fourteen lines. Lost myself in slow bars.

When blood began spilling out of the many eyes of skyscrapers there wasn't anyone to tell me it would be alright. A few kids made clots into red snowmen on our road; I thought about prisons made of iron. The streetlights went out.

Someone disconnected the main arteries, chopped the M1 in to two pieces. Made people drive all the way around Cheltenham to get back to it. The heartbeat slowing to the dull little sound of a pigeon knocking. A city for the spiders to wrap and consume. Everything sleeping in dust.

I am starting to notice the quiet. The lack.

Bird wings fluttering, cold callers, Frank Turner, a cough on a bus, oranges rolling, the sigh of slippers, sweat in the air, the squeal of window wipers, my mother's laughter, Counting Crows, exclamations as vehicles pass through puddles next to pavements, John Martyn, the hum of neon signs, the tiny click of cutting a fingernail, air conditioners, rain sodden fabrics, stubbing toes, Leonard Cohen, a solo piano wire trembling, hair being brushed, waking up suddenly, reaching - my own voice.

Nothing But

It started with the squelch, clunk, pop! of dislocating a knee.
Free of meat and ligament,
the ivory candy-apple of my joint shone; and I bit down.

Marrow-mouthed, I peeled the top of my foot.
It spat in the frying pan and sizzled into leather.
I plucked the tendons on the top like a lyre,
whilst blood splattered percussion on the tiles.
Deboned and declawed, I ripped the music right out of it.
Unsteady, struggling to stand long enough to fry,
I slipped on my way back to the dinner table.

Crunching down to the architecture of myself
I was chewier than I expected myself to be.
Raising my feet to slow the blood loss, I eyed
the curve of my calf.
The huge chunk of fat seemed appealing, at last –
I had waited a lifetime for that feeling.

I sawed the muscle off the bone with a hacksaw.
It sat on the kitchen table like a giant duck breast,
whilst I, leg in a bucket, tore it apart.
Spooned out fat, sat jelly in a bowl.
I would use this fat to fry a kidney! A cube of liver,
a dram of spinal fluid on top – I dreamed of garnish.

Blood-loss blurry, I ate and ate until my stomach roiled,
a tempest captured tight in a carrier bag,
swollen, a fat leech inside of me.
I tugged it out and split it,
so it could dry into blood sausage casing.

Dumped all I had digested on the floor,
alongside piles of cartilage discards.

Things were getting far too messy.
I didn't have a stomach to turn anymore but even so,
the sight of myself spread
so lavishly about the place put me off my food.

So out came the eyes, speared with lollipop sticks
popped and swallowed.
Without eyes or stomach the rest was a breeze.
I ate the rattle in my teeth, ate the retching,
my nose, a lung, a heart relished slow,
slid into the creeping lake of stomach acid
stretching its embrace across the floor to me.
The fizzing of neurons sung to me as they melted,
thought folding in on itself,
a black hole collapsing
disjointed from everything, the last
light dying on the tip of a tongue.

The Moon (Part I & II)

I

And what if you woke up one mint-green morning
and tucked under your duvet beside you was The Moon?
It's sly silver smile wins you over.
You find your eyes sneaking another look,
and every few minutes you gasp, newly astonished again,
mouth overfilled with wonder,
and say, 'wow, look! The moon!'

The moon does not blink at this.
It has heard all of this before.
Sat squat in the bathtub,
the moon is a sharp, protruding bone
that a giant might pick its tar-stained teeth with.
You smooth warm water over it
and notice how it feels so brittle in your hands.

It's probably, I think, that a person would quickly get sick
of the moon.
Ever changing, but stoicly the same.
Always ethereal but never willing to give you more
than the second-hand light it steals from the sun.
You long to sleep alone, eventually.

So you snap the moon.
One night you suddenly feel the vacuum seal
of silence around you both,
and the urge rises to stamp on its great blank face, turn it to ash.
You chip bits off and sell it as star dust on the internet.
Tell yourself that everyone should own a piece of the moon.

You tie the pieces to the roof of your car,
take it to an Easter half term car boot sale
it's almost full; plump and ripe for someone to pick it.
To want it. Like you did before it was with you every night.
Before you grew sick of those tidal displays of its affections
so suddenly swept out with the undercurrent
of tension that comes from cosmic beings
that only manage to exist in the dark.

You untangle yourself from the suffocating silence of the moon.
and tell yourself that you will not miss the smile of it.

II

My father was the moon once.

I remember watching seasons pass over his face
like a stop motion animation
behind the glass of our living room door
waxing and waning endlessly.
I'd come home to bone-white plates
round and empty
staring at me, wondering
why I continued to ask them for things
that they did not have to give me.

I drew pictures of the moon and played dress up.
Painted my face with watercolours pretending I was a rainbow.
I forgot moons and rainbows never meet.
Or perhaps I didn't forget.
Perhaps I picked it so I could tell myself that this was On
Purpose.
Now I have control of the sky.
Now I get to decide how pretty I am
and how often people look or don't look at me when I'm crying.

Maybe I learned how to shrink from my father.
Learned how to make a house in the hollowness of space
that stretches on infinitum between us.
I am not trying to push you away, I just don't have a
gravitational pathway,
Merely pulled from place to place by the habits of being hung
alone in a char black sky.
Depression trims me thin into a scythe, I never wanted to be sharp.
But I understand if you feel like a satellite does not love you enough
if it doesn't revolve around you.

My father used to be the moon.

My mother said it was unlucky to look at a new moon through a
window
and back then, I never listened.
Why risk missing the time the moon was looking back at me?
That rare smile that shone through the space between us,
and a glass-paned door, like Pride.
That warmed the heart like Home.

After all, why have the moon held captive
if you're not going to ask it for lullabies
hoping
that eventually it would say
yes.

Six AM

I lie on a too comfortable sofa and stare
up at a rented chandelier
as Autumn light dies
against the plastic and Winter drips
down fake crystal.

My melancholy is draped
decoratively across furniture
like psychoanalysis is on trend
this season, but I'm itchy.

I know where the wallpaper kisses
its neighbour. The dirty secrets
of the street. I know what happens when
the clock passes six fifty-nine.
It's Six AM again.

I've mapped past tenants' lives from lying here.
Seeing where shadows paint and dirt smudges.
The well-worn hardwood flooring and its pacings,
the curve of door jamb where fretting hands go
when they peer into the gloom to check I am still there.

I am still here.

I could tell you where spiders go to cry.
You'd be surprised.

All through the day and night, Six AM
skitters over me, crawling.

I pluck its droppings off my midday
tea. Flick it away
until the sun zips itself back
into its sleeping bag
and another sunset spills over my coffee table.

I let it stain. Watch it darken.

The Sea

The sea bows its head,
curtseys,
steps back a little in a feigned sign of deference
but her throat rolls and rolls
consonants over continents,
her murmur of dissent;
a warning.
This smile has teeth as sharp as shipwrecks
but it lures me closer anyway.

An Unfinished Apology

Mum,
I'm sorry for all the times I walk out into roads without looking.

I'm sorry my housemates found me on the lip of the river, looking down into its throat, kissing the reality of drowning. It felt like the water wanted to know if I was okay and I just wanted to tell it the truth. It was like all those times you dashed across two cities to see me and muffled everything down to a hushed concern.

I was just writing poetry on the surface Mum. I wanted to write in the black with my body, I wanted to flail and thrash and fight. I wanted to want to survive. I'm sorry I used my feet to write you another suicide note, that I didn't have a better way to tell you this. I know you taught me how to read and write but this monster only speaks to me in agony, and I don't know how to translate for you, I'm sorry.

I've never been a mother; I don't know what its like to have my child hate one of the only perfect things I ever made. I can only imagine how helpless you feel when you find me with the tide lines up my arms; markers of where I was the last time depression flooded me.

I'm trying to remember everything you said to me: just survive the next few minutes, just breathe, just be. I drag my body from the pits and spit out the river water; I repeat and I remember.

Depression's not my home. It's just where I'm living right now, and I know it doesn't make sense but I keep going back there.

Depression has such a welcoming house, Mum. It throws the most beautiful parties. You should hear the stories it tells. Or better yet, I wish I could hear anything else. I wish I could promise that would be the last time.

This poem's not finished. I'm not sure how it ends yet.

The water's cold again. I'm really sorry, Mum.

A Meeting

The river reflected the sky,
dull as a mortuary slab,
laid flat and not breathing at all
as I considered. Consequently,
a water-ward wanderlust quivered in me,
a half-lit thought born as the weak sun hung
and withered away to a eulogy.
Under moon-cut clouds I met with that river.
Toe-shy and too-cold colliding,
I tried to paint myself as a murky mirror,
a reflection, a hasty mirage.
I am not a river. I am sod and clump and clot.
The residue of something beguiling
found convulsing at the bankside;
still alive.

I STILL KEEP THE JEANS THAT I WORE INTO THE RIVER, NOW THICK WITH THE SEDIMENT OF MY MISTAKES. I LIKE TO PRETEND THAT THIS IS THE SAME THING AS REGRET.

Nettles

One time, I was walking across Windsor Bridge,
looking down into the river I have so often dipped my feet in,
and I saw the sky tipped upside down
spilled out all over my city.
And I thought, *how beautiful.*
I told you that the way that the river is always half full,
shimmying at the riverbank edge,
makes me feel like it's optimistic of me to want to be a part of it.

You called me a dumbass. And that was fair.

But this time my eyes passed over grave slate grey water onto
the green, got caught up in the foliage forest of nettles there.

Nettles. Eurgh. I thought. *I can't kill myself there, I'll get stung!*

I told you all of this as I lay fully clothed in an ice bath.
A stupid little story to stop my mind disassociating whilst it was
fixating on the bottle of bathroom bleach too close to me.

*It's like all the times I went to self-harm and cut my fingers on the razor
when I was trying to break it apart. And I'm like, wow, rude, it only
counts if I do it on purpose, piece of crap razor...*

You don't think it's funny. And that's fair.

*It's like the time when I decided I couldn't kill myself because it was my
new flatmate's birthday, so I made a birthday cake like there weren't
three hundred mistakes left to make on my desk.*

Apparently, it's ridiculous to prioritise a near-stranger's birthday
over your own mental breakdown.
But when I say *sorry*,
a word that bubbles out of me, lying here swollen with the want
of river water, and with being alive holding onto me
like a fistful of stinging needles,
you know what I'm apologising for, and just tell me help is on
the way.

That's annoying.
I sulk and turn my face to let the water smother it.
And somehow from two-hundred-odd miles away you help save
me.

And I am freezing cold and shaking but I manage to remember
to say *Thanks for   nothing.*
and you say you'd do anything to keep me here a little while
longer, hoping it would get better and I tell you that
you are Nettles.

A nuisance on the cusp of something.

But later I remember that I am grateful
for all the little obstacles that kept me alive long enough to be
ungrateful for them.
Long enough for scar tissue to grow over the hurt,
for my terror-stricken heart to drum
thank you, thank you, thank you
into my ungrateful, surviving brain.

Cemetery Flowers

Poppies have blossomed under my skin,
blackberries stained the underside
like childhood t-shirts.
I press firmly, the bruise blooms.
I could be the most luscious garden,
cut open, roots exposed I could grow you
such a picturesque memorial ground,
fertilise it myself. I could be
so beautiful.

Sunburnt

We sit in a summer-drenched garden
and pick baby flies off of wrists and thighs.
You, exasperated, sigh. Again.

It makes me laugh which makes you laugh
and buzzings slide away into nothing as we giggle
into coffee mugs
full of own brand lemonade.

We're here to worship the sun.
Here to get warm off of each other's conversations and
compassion
and find the strength to stumble on.

The petunias are posturing for attention,
but your arm is slung over your eyes.
You aren't out here for the sights
you want to absorb more sunshine.

Like you aren't already a blinding force.

Grass seeds slipping between stitch seams
and aggravating the hay feverish flush creeping
across your flesh.

You tell me   'it's hot'.
and I 'mmm' agreeably and try to decide if the shapes we see in
clouds are a correlation of our mental state.

I hope for a tentative smile in the sky.

A grasshopper plays the violin to me.

So, I turn to look at the underside of the petal skirts of
daisies and I listen to a sound more like hazy than humming.

A noise like calm.
I listen to the calm.

And you say:
   'if you don't want to live anymore –

     I guess I get it. It's okay.

     As long as you don't, like,
      keep talking about it'.

I cry until the light hangs behind the horizon on a noose
and the sunburn leaves a permanent scar.

THE GARDEN SENSES ROT BEFORE THE NOSE DETECTS IT. YOU MAKE DAYS FEEL LIKE SUMMER. CANDLELIGHT MAKES ME THINK OF FUNERALS. I HAVE STOPPED LOOKING OVER MY SHOULDER FOR THE SHADOW OF MYSELF. SOMETIMES I FORGET TO TRIP OVER MYSELF WHEN WE'RE DANCING. A TINY SLIPSTEAM INTO ANOTHER PLANE OF EXISTENCE: I CAN HEAR SOMETHING OTHER THAN THESE INTRUSIVE THOUGHTS.

"AS LONG AS YOU DON'T TALK ABOUT IT."

I DID THIS. WHAT'S WRONG SO OBVIOUS? HOW DOES EVERYBODY KNOW? I KNOW I TALK TOO MUCH. LET ME WRITE THIS DOWN ON THE CAVE WALLS OF MY AORTA. IN THE SEDIMENT OF SORROW. LET ME HALF BURY IT IN THE BREAK IN MY VOICE BOX. I WON'T EVER FORGET AGAIN. I DON'T KNOW HOW I AM SUPPOSED TO CLOSE MY EYES AFTER THIS. HOW WILL I EVER LEARN TO KISS WITH A MOUTH FULL OF MY OWN BLOOD?

The Siren Song

Light refracts through the water,
twisting the shape of each shadow floating downstream.
This slow tide tells me riverbedtime stories as lullabies.

I've visited this oil spill far too often.
Settled under the black, with tar-coated optimism:
my sertraline, fluoxetine, venlafaxine --

I've stashed my heart under the river's tongue,
embedded in a siren song that calls me to shipwreck here
so often that the edge of the water is shaped to me.

The song says I belong in the ice-haze.
Days regrow fresh gloom in jellied film,
fingers bloody with picking at cataracts each morning.

Clouds, rolling thin light between them like chewed gum,
diffuse the sun and disperse it on the bankside.
Hope is a fishhook in my throat, it hurts when I swallow.

Wet and river-wild, fingers cracking trachea,
I suffocate all the sorry parts
that the river says are suffocating me.

Limbs too heavy to drag to safety,
I have drowned
and I have died here.

They find my corpse by the canalside
with my tongue swollen out of my mouth.
They assure me that I can talk to them.

but next moonbreak I'm waist deep again.
Relenting to the undercurrent,
and the way cold numbs the nettling in my skin.

I start to believe I belong here. Mermaidic.
That all I can do is try to learn how to stay afloat,
hold my breath and make home in the sediment.

Even debris can be shelter in a storm
and once I let my eyes adjust to the murk
I might find that this is just a deeper blue

and even the darkest colour is just light
trying
to be let back in.

A Letter to Parliament
or 'The Austere Beauty of Trying Not to Die'

The doctors tell me that there is no funding for the services to keep me alive. They send me home to stop my sodden shoes dripping river water in their waiting rooms, they say I'm lucky I have family to stop me. Lucky, I stopped. Unlucky that I stopped in time that I don't quite qualify as an emergency. They say they hope I'll survive and that they are sorry. I am prescribed my small dose of best wishes and that is all between me and memorial.

They say no man is an island. But I am a gay, disabled, working class, woman. And these days in the UK I feel more shorelines than sure thing and making it to tomorrow takes a whole lot more than digging in when the ground keeps shuddering.

This whole chunk of land, uttering its last rite prayers, wondering if it will be enough to stop us sinking. 130,000 of us buried at sea. Thinking ourselves tucked away safely on coastlines quickly subsiding as we sleep, forever peaceful under the scratch-blankets of austerity.

I can no longer afford to romanticise democracy, mental health services that cease to be, or the decades I have spent lost on this seascape of suicidality that my government now hopes will silence me.

I can no longer afford to romanticise it as an ocean at night. Thick with black, curling up at the edges and licking with an unwelcome insistence at the horizon. Blunt as trauma, a blindfold, an eyes gouged out with plastic spoons whose handles snapped half way through, a dark as deep as the hollow of myself in which I have swallowed a sky-full of hope and felt nothing but the bloated toad nausea of the incoming inability to run from danger.

I can no longer pretend I see the moon dropping silver kisses upon crest tips, diamond dusting the blade of each wave.

I can no longer dream of the silence of the sea. Not now. Not when I can feel the full force of physics plotting against me, not when I know that every molecule wants to crash over me, crack through me, crate and bury me - Not when I've been lured to rest my head on riverbeds so often that one of my ears is still full of its' poisonous sludge.

I remember everything that drowning taught me, so I will no longer pretend I am lost on a beautiful seascape, waiting for sirens to tell me my fate as the stars show me how to get home.

The stars are candles extinguished by sea spray. The moon is a gunshot wound in the gut of midnight. The sea and I are no longer lovers.

You are trying to kill me. I will not turn your violence into poetry.

I will no longer believe in sunrises I have never seen. Like hope. Or recovery. Just the ice bite touch of this murderous *blue* water, my half-a-boat floating, and me, trying not to freeze to death and ignoring my MP referring to me as 'Just another person who refused to learn how to swim on their own'.

Reassurances

```
If  you are suffering,  you should know that you can talk to me.
If            suffering,  you should                     talk to me.

If  you                               know that you can talk to me
                          you should                     talk        .

If  you are suffering
                          you should                     talk to me.

I            suffer                                                 .
I                                                can talk
              s          o                   you can       to
                                                            o       .

If  you are suffering,            know that
I            suffer                     t   o           o           .
                                              you can talk to me.

If  you                       d   o
                              no  t             talk to me
                     , you                  can
             suffer  ,
If  you
       are
             suffering                                              .

             suffering    should know
                              h   ow t   o          talk            .

                                            you can talk to me
                          you should know that                      .

                          you         know      you can talk to me
   you are suffering                                                .
             suffer                                                 .
```

Frenchay Hospital, 2008

The on-duty psychiatrist says;

"I know you didn't really want to hurt yourself.
It was just a cry for attention.
Because if you really wanted to die then
you wouldn't have just ▮▮ ▮▮ .
You knew that wouldn't work,
there are far better ways to do it.

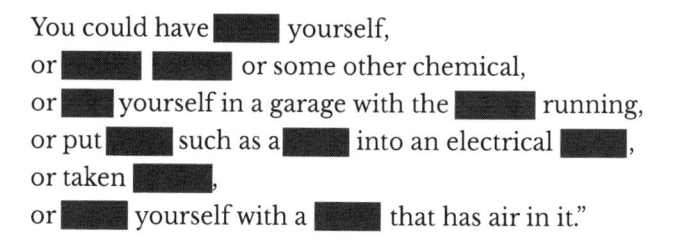

You could have ▮▮ yourself,
or ▮▮ ▮▮ or some other chemical,
or ▮▮ yourself in a garage with the ▮▮ running,
or put ▮▮ such as a ▮▮ into an electrical ▮▮ ,
or taken ▮▮ ,
or ▮▮ yourself with a ▮▮ that has air in it."

He sends me home, an open wound.

PIP2 by the Department of Work and Pensions

This is a found poem, created entirely from words found, in this order, in the Personal Independence Payment application form from 2018.

To help you, we give you time to form an end to your disability.

In space your health conditions are approximate.

Prepare fresh, peeling things sometimes.
Perching light and easy, indicators help vary good and bad days!

Cook pain, help, need. Put in your mouth and swallow.

You don't manage.
Treatments include mental pain and sometimes tablets.

Another person manages your bad days; breathless, tired, monitor you bathing.
Limbs, underarms and hair, standard.
Provide something grab safe: your body parts!

Do you, either during or after the activity, like pain?

Have the person tell you when to use the toilet, watch over you, condition you.

Tell us you can manage.

You can dress yourself in shoes and clothes and boxes that apply to you. Select change.
It takes the day of your body parts dressing and undressing to help you understand.

Your native language: symbols and need.
Sign language helps by speaking on your behalf.
You don't get to communicate.
Reading these questions, you can understand dates, instructions, information spectacles and sometimes words.

Tell us about good, complicated pain.
Face towards appropriate anxiety.
Difficulties you have put others at risk.
Bad times cost you.

Follow a route to severe anxiety. Stress prevents you.
Know, we mean you need help.
You need to be encouraged to have a dog.

Lost somewhere you don't know well?
Sometimes to go out reassures you, but don't go out.
Severe anxiety completes you.

Next, we contact you face-to-face.
If you've given us enough, we ask you to attend a consultation on health.
It's not a full physical examination, but the health professional will understand your life.

We cannot pay you; the returned form may have a penalty that may affect independence.

The Department for Work and Pensions collects an allowance for schemes.

We may get you.

The law allows us to do so.

Halo

A halo of rope around my neck
is the closest to heaven that I'll ever get.

The Last Light

After the lung shivers around a globule
of fluid, rattling to dismiss it.
After hallucination and disorientation,
after the tears and words,
far after these poor man's indicators
of consciousness have passed.
After the kidney droops raisin'd, bowing
its head on its wilting stalk.
After the tepid heart brushes its vibrato
through the body for a final time
and the resonance of that note dully hums
through the mottled skin.
After the blurry murmurs
of a destituted loved-one fades to tinnitus.
After it becomes nothing but sound
(and then to nothing as much as that),
as the brain itself claws the inside
of a skull for the semblance of a breath;
in the tipping moment between that and
the culmination of a life well grown;
only then will hope,
the last one to turn out the light inside,
die.

Uric Acid

Some people have depression like gout.
Like uric acid forming needles in the blood
and pooling in the joints.
Some people have depression
like the aortic valve rupturing,
like the ripping of muscle into pear halves.
And both are agony.

But it's lonely when people step back
so they don't get bloodrush on their shoes
and ask what's wrong with me.
I don't know, I shrug, it was like this when I got here.

WHAT'S WRONG WITH YOU?

IT WAS LIKE A BURDEN WHEN I GOT HERE

BUT IT ISN'T DOESN'T KNOW

Meeting Magic

We met in a smoky pub that had magician shows on weeknights.
You had a smile that tore rabbits out of hats,
I wanted to do magic like that.
I befriended you in front of the swing doors to the toilet stalls
and we exchanged nerves and names at the bar.
You read that funny bathroom poem
and the audience heard your sadness before you admitted
to yourself that that's what it was.
That sometimes what feels like love is just the saddest line
in a poem, stuck in your mind forever.

You told me that octopuses have nine minds
and I wondered if they were all equally responsible
for bodily functions.
I wondered when some were sleeping what it must be like to
feel 1/9th drowning
and also wholly like your lungs are filling with cold water.
You never liked the cold water.
Told me that in Cyprus the sea was the warm bath
you have while you wait for the cops to save you,
in those small moments between silence and safety.
How that sea was a horizon, was hope, was a pathway here.
How the sea held you as a child
before you felt like you were a crime you didn't commit.
Before you committed what you didn't know was a crime.
Before basement blues and flavoured vodka and colouring
your hair became a substitute for feeling.
Before dancing was limbs chattering
telling all the theatre your secrets.
Before the feeling of being washed out with the tide
and the feeling of being left behind on the sand collided

into one perfectly sad line in some song, or some poem you
loved about something bigger than you.

You stood, chin up, trying to drink from the spike
of the nearest star,
and I asked if drinking silver and spotlight
would help us take over the world.
And you said the world was already ending;
spinning so fast onto a path of self-destruction tattooed onto
your inner thigh,
a map of place names and people who guarantee implosion.
You said that the forests were already burnt out.
You'd shown them how.
But we were clinging on so tightly that it felt like nothing
was moving and that this would be the last
closest thing to quiet at the end of the world.

I told you I was the ending.
I knew this because I was the saddest thing in all of my poems.
You threw your shoes into the tree outside the Birmingham
Hippodrome and said

        'Then for fucks sake, write about something else!'

Then you twirled round and round and round
until the stars became perfect circles,
a halo above you;
and I laughed until my lungs turned midnight.

Growing

In the thick of the forest,
under the barbed-wire bracken
in its curves and coils
of bramble and dagger-knife nubs unsheathed.

Beneath those thorny waves
in the undercurrent of dusk and moss
and the trapped smell of rotting things
that are feeding other things.

Tucked under fallen logs, haphazard
diagonal slashes across pathways -
freckled with fungi forming blushed buttons.
Just nestled neatly under that

and under the compressed grass
and roots peaking up, tubular brains
wriggling to look blindly up at the green sky.
Beneath loose soil and sod

and most of the skeleton of a long-gone mouse,
arranged as an earthbound bouquet.
Just there, clumped with clod and rainwater
life slices sharp through the dark and rises

having split the earth open just a crack -
it's enough.

Ways of Coping With A Personality Disorder Distorting How Your Brain Processes Reality And Making You Really Fucking Miserable

You have to earn change
by scraping two days together
and surviving them.
Endure today.
They cannot "Fix" you
overnight. Maybe ever.
This poem can't undo the black
and heavy that has its foot
on your throat.

If you have found a root, share it.
This Forest is so dark.
Scuff the dirt so someone knows you
came this way.
Your long-gone
footprints might be enough
to guide the others.
We make the path by walking it.

Peony-Bruised

I lie down in a bath brim-filled with peonies
and feel their soft crush beneath my weight.
That soundless collapse of a teen girl.
The emptiness of discarded velvet dresses.
Pink blood blot tests me where I move,
my thigh is a map of a country in lockdown;
see how it doesn't move but it can tremble.
This city is a bruise I keep pressing upon
so I dip myself under and ask the petals
to tell me their first memories.

Rain,
they say.

Rain.

And then, how we grew.

ACKNOWLEDGEMENTS

Cliff Notes was developed with funding from Arts Council England, and I must thank John Berkavitch, Sven Stears and Sadie Davidson for the encouragement, advice and inspiration to apply for it. This funding helped make this collection the best that it could be, and I am forever grateful for that opportunity.

Stuart Bartholomew, thank you for believing in me before I believed in myself and letting me become part of the VERVE family. It is a true honour.

This collection would be twice as long and half as meaningful without the immense generosity of passion and time shared with me by Caroline Bird, Tina Sederholm, Rachel Long, Jemma Hathaway and Anthony Anaxagorou. Each of these incredible artists contributed huge ideas or tiny details of their insight and made a huge impact on the way these poems evolved. I must also thank those generous souls who gave their time to read and give feedback on this collection at various stages: Anne Gill, Elizabeth McGeown, Chris Cambell, Jasmine Gardosi, Amy Acre, Talya Stitcher and Shane Koyczan. I cannot thank any of you enough.

Caroline, our weekly sessions were the spine of this journey and kept me to feel like I was continuously growing and getting this collection closer and closer to what I dreamt it could be. I am so grateful to have had the opportunity to learn from you and benefit from your wisdom and kindness. I will never be able to thank you enough.

I would like to thank all those who helped develop individual poems that appear in the collection. Including facilitation spaces held by Cecilia Knapp, Apples and Snakes (Red Sky Sessions), UniSlam, Lyra Fest, and courses I attended run by

The Poetry School and Arvon. Specifically, Caroline Bird for the space in which I wrote 'Bowl', 'Hired Mourner'. Anthony Anaxagorou and my classmates at The Poetry School for the space in which I wrote and developed 'Camaraderie' and 'Diminuendo'. Bohdan Piasecki, Rachel Long, John Berkavitch and the Red Sky Sessions for the space in which I wrote 'Laurac Le Grand, 1992', 'Anaphora' and 'I Kiss Like Church'. Cecilia Knapp for the space in which I wrote 'Dorchester Hospital' and the inspiration which turned into 'The Moons (Part I & II). Liv McCaughey for the prompt that sparked the poem 'The Little Things'. Raina Greifer for the space in which I wrote 'Lockdown, 2004 - 2012'. Raymond Antrobus and Arvon for the space in which I wrote 'The Recovery Position'. Rhys Trimble and The Poetry School for the space in which I wrote 'Reassurances'. Toby Campion, Ben Norris and my UniSlam family for the space in which I wrote 'Meeting Magic'.

The following poems first appeared in these amazing literary homes: 'The Siren Song' in *The Dizziness of Freedom* by Bad Betty Press. 'Disorderly Conduct' in *404 ink magazine* and *UniSlam 2019 Anthology*. 'Lockdown, 2004 - 2012' in *SLAMMinutes does Mental Health in the Pandemic*. 'Sunburnt' in *UniSlam 2021 Anthology*. 'Found' in Sanctuary by Woodend/Dream Well Publishing. 'Tracey Emin Got Nothin' On Me' in *ISOLA*. 'The Moons (Part I & II)' in *The Open Collab* by Charlie and Jake. 'A Letter to Parliament' by *Muddy Feet Poetry* and *Process Productions*. 'An Unfinished Apology' by *Inkbomb*.

It would be remiss of me not to thank some of the people who have given me great opportunities and guidance in the poetry and spoken word world. I would not have found this pathway without the kindness of Lucy English, Danny Pandolfi (and the Raise the Bar team), Malaika Kegode (and the Milk team), Tyrone Lewis and Jake Wild Hall (and the Boomerang team), Clive Oseman and Nick Lovell (and the Oooh Beehive family), John Paul O'Neill, Toby Campion (and the UniSlam team), the members of the Bath Spa poetry team for the past six years,

Steve Larkin (and the Hammer & Tongue team), the production, cast and crew of Life and Rhymes, Liv Torc, Bryce Kahari (and my Poetry Battles family), the Full House Literary Magazine team (especially JP and Leia), and Apples and Snakes.

But more importantly I have to thank the people who helped me distinguish between intrusive thoughts, imposter syndrome and the truth. Fay Roberts, Melanie Branton, Thommie Gillow, Shagufta K Iqbal, Shaun Hill, Rebecca Cooney, Raina Greifer, Sophia Kaniklidou, Sam J. Grudings, Sanket Shrestha, Cathi Rae, Beth Hartley, Matthias Ediger, Ken Cumberlidge, Dee Dickens, Joelle Taylor, Alex Calver, Helen Sheppard, Chris Beale, Beth Calverley, Josie Alford, Michael Wilson, Rick Dove, Tom Dewey, Jah-Mir Early, Polly Denny, Claire Guest, Chloë Jacquet, Bex Gordon, Holly Moberley, Em Murray, Rose Butler, Amy Stirling, the 'poetlings', and everyone who has ever taken the time to give me a kind word, you made all the difference in the world.

It has taken too many people to name to keep me alive thus far, in order to be here to write this collection. Please know that if ever you have been a friend to me, I remain grateful to you to this day no matter when we last spoke. With that said, special thanks to my most treasured friends: Antonia, Jon (Nettles), Daniel, Nina, Nick, Caduceus, Lisa, Connor, Rohan, Rhi, Katie, George, Cal, Tyjana, Robyn, Kris, Charlie, Maiku, Robert, Simon, Sarah, Di, Becky, Luke, Beth K., Nicole, Gareth, Fay, Nina (Bethan), Kirsty, Shane, Sven, Laura-Marie, Jasper, Vinny, Laika and Sir. They are not the only ones who have kept me alive, but they have all individually helped me keep my head above water in a way that I can never repay them for.

My final and most sincere thanks to all of my family. To Jemma, for scouting out poetry bookshops on my behalf, reading countless drafts, and having faith in me all along. To my Dad, for always encouraging me to get lost (and found) in words. To every single one of them who has put up with me writing poems since primary school. For your continued patience and understanding that my poems reflect my perspective, and not an absolute truth, and for allowing me the space to express it.

To my mum and my beloved fiancée Kasha-Faye, thank you for standing in the dark with me when we couldn't find a way out. You both know that I wouldn't be here if it wasn't for you two. I owe you both everything. I am continuously humbled by your love and strength. I wouldn't want to be apart of any other team.

and finally, to Laura.
May this keep you alive, at least between these pages.

ABOUT VERVE POETRY PRESS

Verve Poetry Press is a quite new and already award-winning press that focused initially on meeting a local need in Birmingham - a need for the vibrant poetry scene here in Brum to find a way to present itself to the poetry world via publication. Co-founded by Stuart Bartholomew and Amerah Saleh, it now publishes poets from all corners of the UK - poets that speak to the city's varied and energetic qualities and will contribute to its many poetic stories.

Added to this is a colourful pamphlet series, many featuring poets who have performed at our sister festival - and a poetry show series which captures the magic of longer poetry performance pieces by festival alumni such as Polarbear, Matt Abbott and Genevieve Carver.

The press has been voted Most Innovative Publisher at the Saboteur Awards, and has won the Publisher's Award for Poetry Pamphlets at the Michael Marks Awards.

Like the festival, we strive to think about poetry in inclusive ways and embrace the multiplicity of approaches towards this glorious art.

www.vervepoetrypress.com
@VervePoetryPres
mail@vervepoetrypress.com